MAKE HIM

WANT

YOU BAD

Tantalizing Secrets to Make
Your Boyfriend Love You
More, Make Him Commit, and
Never Leave You at All

Jennifer G. Sorensen

Author's Note

This publication is designed to provide insightful information in regards to the subject matter covered. It is sold with the understanding that neither the author nor publisher is engaged in rendering psychological, medical, or other professional services. If expert assistance or counseling is needed, seek the services of a competent professional.

While many experiences related in this book are authentic, names and identifying details have been changed to protect the individuals' privacy.

TABLE OF CONTENTS

INTRODUCTION

How do I drive my boyfriend crazy this is a question we all ask ourselves when we find ourselves falling helplessly in love with the guy we are dating. Our dream is that he feels the same as do. Most of us leave this to fate or chance, but it's not really the best course of action.

Getting a man to love you more has a lot to do with who you are and how you treat him.

Relationships take work, but making improvements doesn't have to be a painful task. Even small changes in your communication and interaction can turn your romance from sweet to stratospheric. Let's go into details on how to make your boyfriend love you more.

CHAPTER ONE

Improve Your Communication

Avoid Taking Your Friend For Granted.

After being together for a while, it's normal for the two of you to take each other for granted. This is one of the typical challenges in relationships these days, but it doesn't have to ruin yours.

Try to think about the things you love about your boyfriend several times a week. Maybe that's why he knows exactly when you've had a bad day and gives you pizza and a movie. Maybe he's also good at volleyball. Whatever you like about him, do your best to think about it. It's also a good idea to tell your friend what is so good about him every now and then.

But don't take this to the other extreme and become over-clingy, though.

Constantly reviewing everything he does to see if he "really" loves you will only make you anxious and stressed out. If he says he loves you and his actions usually back it up, keep in mind that everyone slips out from time to time; take his word for it.

Be An Active Listener.

It can be easy to change conversations, especially when you don't feel like doing it or are distracted by your own things. It happens to everyone. Learn to take notes as you stretch and practice "active listening" instead. Your friend will feel more valued and appreciated, and you might learn things that you didn't know.

Review and clarify what you have heard.

This step can always save you many heartaches, especially if you are in an emotional conversation. Instead of assuming you heard correctly, rephrase what you heard and ask for clarification: "Okay, let's see if I heard you correctly. I heard you say _____. Is that correct?" If you didn't get to understand anything he said the first time around, then ask your boyfriend to explain.

To encourage.

It shows that you understand what your friend is saying. Ask short questions like "What happened next?" or "What did you do?" You can notify by nodding your head and using a minimal encourager, just like "Uh-huh" or "Oh".

To summarize.

When you have had a conversation with a lot of information, summarize the main topics. This shows that you are paying attention and allows for optimization or feedback. "Okay, so you are pretty worried because you've got a really stressful day at work tomorrow, and you want me to come to pick you up and go to the arcade tomorrow night." I'm I right?"

These techniques are more than romantic relationships! You can improve your communication with anyone.

Ask Questions.

It's not just "What did you do today?" or "What do you want to eat?" Asking meaningful and curious or probing questions can improve your conversations. I may help each other to share your feelings and thoughts. In fact, studies have shown that asking deep questions leads to more intimacy and a sense of being in love.

For example, if your friend talks about a problem with one of their classes, ask a haunting question; like "May I know what you think would happen if you tried _____?"

Avoid Pointing Fingers.

Questions and statements that focus on the "you" and "why" messages can cause problems. These seem accusatory and force the other person to shut down or react defensively.

For example, it's not an excellent idea to ask a question like, "Why do you always forget to pick me up from the office?" This will just make you look accusing and angry and not attractive at all.

Instead, use "I" statements. You can also ask questions that require legitimate information. For example: "I noticed that you weren't there to pick me up as we had decided earlier." It doesn't sound accusatory as long as you stay away from the sarcasm!, But it does communicate your feelings and give your friend a space to share his.

Avoid Sermons.

It is better to leave the preaching work in the pulpit. It's tempting to give advice to others, especially when you're in a relationship. When someone has asked you for advice, offer it. Otherwise, it can be condescending, preaching, or as if you don't trust the other person enough to make their own decisions.

When people request advice, they are really looking for someone to listen to them with a listening ear. If you think this is happening to your boyfriend, ask, "Do you just need someone to listen to, or would you like me to try to figure it out?"

Stay away from "should". No one likes to be told you should or shouldn't be doing this. It can make them stupid or condescending. Instead, try something like "How about ____?" or "Have you tried ____?"

Concede Being Right.

It isn't easy. We are all inspired by the desire to be "right," at least sometimes. However, in most situations, there is no straightforward "right" or "wrong." Please don't start a conversation with your friend like it's a fight.

This doesn't imply that you are not entitled to your feelings and thoughts. You do. What you feel is what you think. Remember that your boyfriend is also entitled to his feelings and thoughts. There is no I am "right," or I am "wrong" with emotions. What the two of you can control are your own reactions to emotions.

For example, imagine if your boyfriend walks up to you and tells you that you have embarrassed him in front of his friends. You may think this is totally unfair, but take the time to acknowledge his feelings: "I'm sorry I embarrassed you." Then you can explain your point: "I didn't know that would embarrass you. I won't try to do it again next time."

If you start out defensively, the other person will likely stop listening. If you first acknowledge the other person's feelings and then explain to them if necessary, the other person is more likely to feel validated and accepted that you didn't mean to offend him or her.

Not claiming to be "right" does not mean you have to be a fool. If you think something is noteworthy, speak up. Remember to listen to the other person's point of view as well. A compromise may be the best solution.

Talk About Embarrassing Things.

If you don't share the intimate and sometimes embarrassing thoughts, needs, and feelings you have with each other, your relationship can suffer. Studies show that people who do not openly share their feelings and needs with others do not feel as emotionally secure or generally happy as those who do.

Studies have also revealed that couples who don't communicate openly and directly with each other are more likely to feel insecure about their relationships.

Try not to label your needs or those of your boyfriend as "stupid" or "immature." Dismissal damages confidence. You should both feel that the other is a safe person to share even the scariest things with.

Don't hide or hide your feelings to "be strong." Suppressing or hiding your feelings can lead to resentment and seriously damage your relationship.

When your friend shares something with you, show that you are listening and empathetic by saying stuff like "I appreciate your willingness to share this with me" or "I hear you saying that you are afraid of ____". These open and acceptable comments will encourage them to see you as someone they can trust.

Keep Passive Aggression Out Of Your Life.

Passive-aggressive behavior is the opposite of clear and open communication and can destroy a relationship in no time. It is usually caused by anger or pain. It can be tempting to "punish" your boyfriend when he is upset or hurt, but it's much healthier (and more effective) to talk about it.

There are so many ways to be passive-aggressive in a relationship, and below are some to watch out for:

Not "remembering" to do something. People exhibit passive aggression in relationships by "forgetting" to do something they don't want to do. You can "forget" to buy tickets for the movie you really don't want to see. He can "forget" your wedding anniversary day if you have hurt him. This type of behavior hurts both of you.

To say things you don't mean to say Sarcasm is a quick way to hurt other people. Sometimes people use passive-aggressive language to indirectly communicate that they are dissatisfied or upset. For example, if your friend forgot you were supposed to have a game together on Friday night and instead bought tickets to a hockey game, a passive-aggressive response might be, "No, why should I be angry?" I love it when you do forget things that are essential to me. You should definitely go to this hockey game. "Rather than conveying your feelings respectfully and clearly, this kind of language creates defense and even confusion (some people just aren't good at addressing Sarcasm).

Displaying the "silent treatment". If you are feeling upset or hurt, you can ignore your boyfriend or pretend you can't hear anything. This type of behavior is detrimental because it can ruin actual attempts to strike up a conversation and ultimately discourage the discussion altogether. If you actually need some time to cool off - which is perfectly healthy and natural - be open about it: "I'm too angry to talk about this now. Please give me an hour or so, and we will talk about it then."

Watch **Your Body Language.**

We communicate more with our non-verbal communication - our body language and gestures - than with what we say. Watch your body language. You might be sending messages that you didn't intend to send.

Don't keep your arms crossed and loose. Crossing your arms across your chest to look defensive or closed.

Make eye contact. Not making eye contact is a great way to let the other person know that you are not involved or that you are not listening to what the person is saying. Endeavor to make eye contact at least 50% of the time when he is speaking and 70% of the time while you are listening.

Avoid pointing. It can be accusing or intimidating. Instead, try making an open palm gesture.

Keep your body facing the other person when interacting. A look away from or to the side of the other person indicates that you are not concerned with what is going on.

Recap.
By communicating your needs, you can better support each other. Just be open about how you feel and what you need, and then agree on how you can show mutual appreciation if that works out well, then the two of you can move forward compatibly together."

CHAPTER TWO

Building Love Through Actions

Ditch The Tech.

We are living in a super connected world, but ironically it can make you and your boyfriend feel more distant. You don't really communicate when you're constantly on your phones and computers. Prepare to have time for both of you: no phones, no computers, no video games.

It is very easy to pick up your phone without even realizing that you have done it; if such is an issue for you, try keeping your phone away from your location, such as a desk or in a box near the door if it's your "no-tech time" together.

If you don't live together, try making a phone or Skype connection in addition to sending text messages. Much of communication involves non-verbal cues such as voice notes, gestures, and facial expressions. All these are lost in the texts. Try to chat as close as possible to "in person" for a few minutes each day. This will help bond him and keep him continuing the intimacy you showed with him at the start.

Fix Your Routines.

Do you recall when you both first started dating, how each date was something new? And you were so happy to see each other that you could hardly wait for a date night? Once you've gotten into a "rut" in your relationship, you might feel happier spending time together by varying your routines.

Try something new. If you try new things together, whether it's a new restaurant or a new hobby, you can immerse yourself in this experience. It will also expand your "toolbox" with fun things to enjoy together.

Change your current routines. For example, if you like movie nights, see what you can do to make them more fun. See if an old movie theater is showing your favorite movie on the big screen. See "Performances under the stars" in summer. Go to a dinner theater or an accompanying movie. Create a themed dinner for your next movie night ("Goodfellas" and spaghetti?).

Find Things That You Both Like.

These don't have to be huge. Even if you do your homework together at a coffee shop, spending time together can help you feel more connected.

Make Sure Your Friend Has Time For Himself.

Relationships work best when the two people have different interests and spend time alone or with their own friends. You both need an identity that is not about the other. No one likes to be constantly watched or moved.

It shows him that you trust him. If you let him know that he deserves your trust, he is less likely to lose that trust. If you don't trust him, he's more likely to betray that trust just because he resents not being trusted.

Regardless of how much you love yourself, no one can meet every other person's single needs. When you hang out with other friends and have outside interests, you can be happy, healthy, and eclectic people all at the same time. It also makes the time you spend together memorable.

Personalize Your Gifts And Outings.

Especially if your friend enjoys receiving gifts or surprises, it personally shows that you know him better than anyone else and that you really care about his needs and preferences. Think about the things your boyfriend loves doing/getting and use them as a guide.

Does your boyfriend like to exercise? Is he an adrenaline junky? Get a pair of tickets to a local soccer, basketball, or football game. Take him to an amusement center and ride as many roller coasters as you can in three hours.

Is your boyfriend the hopeless romantic type? In touch with his sensitive side? Give him an old book of poems by Philip Larkin or John Keats and write something on the cover, just like a vow: "With all my heart - the love that flows through these words is only for you and you alone forever."

Is your boyfriend an outdoors guy? Take him on a camping trip and crawl in his sleeping bag. Or take him with you for whale or bird watching at your local Audubon society.

Leave A Thoughtful Little Note In Your Lunch Or Shirt Pocket.

If your friend likes positive words (do you remember those love words?), Drop them a message. Whether it's simple, humorous, or downright crazy, these little reminders can show you care.

In your note, inscribe something that will make your boyfriend most comfortable. If he's a little nervous about bubbling emotions, leave him a playful and fun note. If he likes real expressions of emotion, let him know how much he means to you.

As we human, we quickly get used to the positive things in our lives. This is called "hedonic adaption". Make sure you don't overdo or leave too many notes that they don't make sense or meaning anymore. Too many of a good thing really is still too much.

Show Your Affection.

Expressing affection is especially important if your boyfriend values "physical touch" as the language of love. Don't do anything that bothers him; just let him know you think he's cute.

See what your boyfriend likes. Maybe he likes it when you bite his neck, or maybe he hates it. Knowing why he feels loved and what turns him on is a healthy way to show your affection.

Wearing your "sexy" clothes for your boyfriend can spice up your relationship and love. Figure out if he has a fantasy or something he likes and does something special every now and then. He will happily reciprocate the favor.

Remember that there are other ways to show physical affection besides sex. Also, try holding hands, cuddling, kissing, and hugging. It's good to have different ways of showing affection for each other.

Don't take it personally if your boyfriend doesn't have the same physical display of love like you; people are different.

Go Out With His Your Friends Sometimes.

It's important that you both have different interests and your own friends, but it can also strengthen your relationship by spending time with each other's friends.

A common problem in new relationships is spending more time with your new boyfriend and less time with your friends. It can make your friends feel neglected, and it can also put a strain on your relationship. Integrate your friend into your social circle by inviting them every now and then. Try going out with your friends from time to time also.

Make An Appointment And Go To A Place Where You Can Chat And Relax.

For example, have a quiet dinner and tell your boyfriend how much he means to you. Let him tell you about some of his opinions and feelings. Really listen to what he has to say, but add a comment to expand the conversation. Clear a few things up if necessary.

Go on dates you think he would enjoy. Think about activities where you can be close to each other, for example, A boat trip, a train ride, a nature walk, a trip to the zoo, a day trip to a nearby town, etc.

Play Hooky Together.

Take a day off. Do something completely unexpected, like creating and recording music together. Use your newfound freedom, even if it's only for a day, and live like you have a day to love.

Making memories together can help you remember something later. Research has shown that remembering the fun experiences you had together later on, helps you feel more connected.

CHAPTER THREE

Get To Know Your Friend Better.

Learn To Give And Receive Love.

According to psychologist Gary Chapman, people have a "language of love" with which to show themselves and interpret other people's displays of love. Knowing the language of each other's love can help you show your love in a way that will help the other bond the stronger. If you and your boyfriend have contrasting love languages and you don't know them, it can cause a lot of stress.

The five known languages of love, according to Gary Chapman, are "affirming words", "acts of service", "receiving gifts", "quality time," and "physical touch".

"Confirmation words" are things like praise, encouragement, or "checking" your feelings.

"Service" means things like housework or everyday activities that the other person doesn't like to do.

"Receiving gifts" are things like visible symbols of love like flowers or gifts.

"Quality time" is time or moment spent with your partner without interruptions or distractions.

"Physical contact" can be any manifestation of physical affection, including hugging, kissing, or having sex.

The key to these languages is to share them. This way, if your boyfriend prefers "physical contact" to "receiving gifts," you will know how to show him that you love him in a way that he will bond with. If your boyfriend knows that "receiving gifts" is your primary language, he won't be confused unless you don't typically see his taking out the trash regularly as a sign of love.

It's also important to keep this in mind so that you can pay attention to love languages that you might not otherwise notice.

Find A Balance Between Intimacy, Commitment, And Passion.

These three elements constitute Robert Sternberg's doctrine of love. In general, while psychologists hold different opinions, it is romantic "love" that makes you feel intimate and engaged with a particular person. Passion or lust is a sexual desire that may or may not be limited to one person. In relationships, the urge to feel is often an incentive: if you find someone warm, you will be interested in pursuing them. Love takes time to develop and flourish.

In relationships, it's normal for both emotions to have their ups and downs. At the start of a relationship - often referred to as the "honeymoon phase" - it's very common for desire to come to a peak: you can't hold back and become obsessed with how sexy the other is. Nobody. This is great, but it's also normal for this stage to decrease as you get to know each other better and spend reasonable time together.

Once the first fit of thirst is gone, idealizing your boyfriend because of the chemicals in your brain are going a little bit crazy. If that pedestal comes crashing down, you will notice things that irritate you, like the way he flosses in front of or pays for his groceries differently in the store than you do; this is normal. This is where "love" comes into play. Love offers you the patience to ignore the little annoyances because you really love this guy.

This does not mean that the lust should go away after a few months of dating. Take the time to figure out what turns you and your boyfriend on. Both of you should communicate your sexual needs. Spice up your routines and have fun together!

Realize That People Have Different Styles Of Communication.

"Men are said to come from Mars, whereas women are from Venus," and it is a well-known truth, but the reality is actually more complicated. Even people of the same sex can have very different communication styles. Whether you are gay or straight, and you and your boyfriend sometimes speak other languages, your communication styles may not be the same. Either way, nothing is "better" per se, but understanding how the two of you communicate is helpful.

Some people are affiliative communicators. Affiliative communicators like to solicit feedback from others. They prefer to work together and may see challenges or disagreements as signs of aggression or hostility. If you choose to listen to all parties, avoid conflict, solve problems together, and talk less often, you might be an affiliative communicator.

Some people are competitive communicators. Competitive communicators are generally straightforward, confident, and willing to present challenges. They often like gathering information and make their own verdicts. They usually prefer to be responsible. If you speak your mind readily, comfortable with conflict, and prefer to make your own decisions, you might be a competitive communicator.

People can also differ in their directness. Most people are comfortable with direct communication, such as "I want to spend more time together". Others feel more comfortable with indirect communication, for example: "It is nice to spend time together. It is a shame we don't do it anymore. "Any form can be appropriate depending on the situation. The essential thing is to listen to one another and to clarify when you don't understand.

Different styles of communication don't mean your relationship is doomed. It just means that you need to know what differences can create tension between you and that you need to both engage in flexibility and compromise.

Advice

- Look at yourself and look at your own actions. We can only change ourselves, not others.

- Work with your self-esteem and self-confidence. We can only be fully available to others if we are satisfied with ourselves.

- Show that you trust him and that you love him in your actions. Ascertain that your actions are consistent with what you are saying.

- Say what you mean, and mean what you say. No one can read minds.

- Try to resolve disputes as quickly as possible to avoid lingering resentment. Never make a big deal of minor issues.

- Be yourself around him.

- Tell him "I love you" from time to time.

- Let him know that you are always behind him.

- Don't get angry and chase him when he's with people you don't like.

- Don't get too clingy! Give your partner some space at times if he needs it.

- Always be respectful of him. If he's not ready or wants to spend some time alone, give him some space.

- Learn to say I'm sorry every time you make a mistake.

CHAPTER FOUR

10 Quick Solution

1. Make Yourself Beautiful.

When you look good, you get the attention you need to make him fall in love with you. Most people act on what they see. So, pay attention to what you wear, if your hair is nice or dry, and if you are well dressed. Do your best to be your best wherever you go. Your boyfriend is sure to love you.

2. Be Yourself.

Just take off your mask and let him know that you accept yourself for who you are. Your friend doesn't want to see the fake. If you don't stick with this person for the rest of your life, eventually, he will see the actual you one day. So if you want him to fall in love with you, be yourself from the start. Our authenticity creates a profound intimacy that boys and girls crave.

Also, try to be the best version of yourself. If you stay true to yourself, if you accept your flaws, your guy will fall in love with you because of your honesty and humility. It also gives him the confidence he needs to trust you. But if you want him to fall in love with you now and forever, don't just be happy with who you are right now, especially if you have negative habits and attitudes that might drain your patience in the future. Instead, show him that you are doing your best to grow as a person for your man and the union.

If he loves you sincerely, then he will surely accept you for who you really are, despite your shortcomings and differences. But if you want him to love you more and extend your relationship, do all you can to really improve yourself. Either way, it will make it clear to your boyfriend that you are not only thinking for yourself but also for him and the future of your relationship.

3. Smile And Be Happy.

Remember to enjoy it and show it off as much as you can. The happier you are, the more your boyfriend will be drawn to your positive mood. Oftentimes, flash a natural smile, be enjoyable and pleasant, laughed at his jokes, and be optimistic. Boys generally like girls with a sense of humor who can make them feel good.

4. Be Kind And Considerate.

Always say "thank you" in anything he does for you, be it minor or significant, praise him, give him time or lend him a helping hand. Showing your kind personality increases your man's love for you.

5. Show Your Affection.

Sometimes you have to show someone your love and adoration through your actions. You can do this by really listening to him, doing something nice for him every day, taking your time no matter how busy you are, verbally confirming that you care about him, supporting him and remembering that physical contact can mean a lot.

You can also show him affection by asking him about his day.

If you ask your guy how his day was, he will see how much you care about him, but if you listen to his responses, you'll see how much he will love you. It's just a simple reminder to him that someone cares about both the big and small aspects of his day.

6. Give Him A Physical Touch.

Physical touch is the most essential part of love. Your touch would be incredibly exciting for the man you love. Give him long, tight hugs, passionate kisses, or hold your hands in public. Not only will this make your man happier and feel loved, but it will also reduce his anxiety, improve his mood, and lower his stress levels.

7. Be A Woman Who Values Him.

A man just wants you to appreciate all of his efforts for you. That is really isn't much to ask for. So if you want him to see the best of you and fall desperately in love with you, just cherish him and never take him for granted. Compliment him as much as possible, show respect, encourage his outside interests, thank him, give him time and remind him of minor flaws, but focus on his good qualities.

8. Accept Him For Who He Is.

If you want your man to fall in love with you, accept him for who he is now. Don't see him as some sort of thing to be fixed. Instead, just accept the fact that he's not perfect; he makes mistakes and has flaws.

9. Bring Out The Best In Him.

Guys want a girl who can encourage them to pursue their passion. If you get the most out of him, he'll feel good, and he'll want to be with you. Focus on his strength, intelligence, wisdom, courage, and belief in him more than he believes in himself.

10. Just Love Him.

Finally, love him from the bottom of your heart. Of course, love attracts love. Whatever you do to make him fall in love with you, you can never be successful if you don't fall in love with him first. You shouldn't expect your boyfriend to fall for you in return. So just give him your pure and tender love, and he will, of course, activate his hidden or unreleased love for you.

CONCLUSION

Always remember that you don't have to be perfect to be the best version of yourself just to enable him to fall in love with you. You also don't have to compete with other girls for your boyfriend's love and attention. What you need to do is compete with yourself - to grow as a person - to develop the love you give him - to fall more in love with you without expecting it naturally - and so your relationship and love can become happier and stronger.

Enjoy your relationship – More □

Made in the USA
Coppell, TX
09 April 2022

76277729R00022